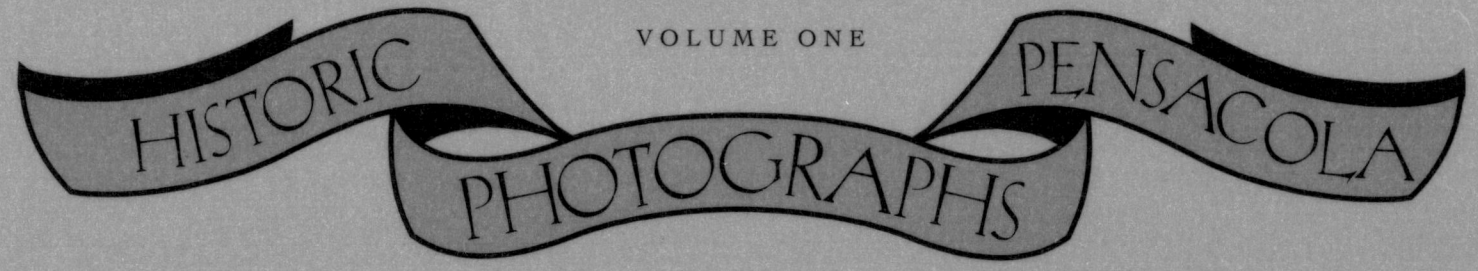

VOLUME ONE

HISTORIC PHOTOGRAPHS PENSACOLA

BayShore PUBLISHING GROUP, INC.
PENSACOLA, FLORIDA

HISTORIC PENSACOLA PHOTOGRAPHS

VOLUME ONE

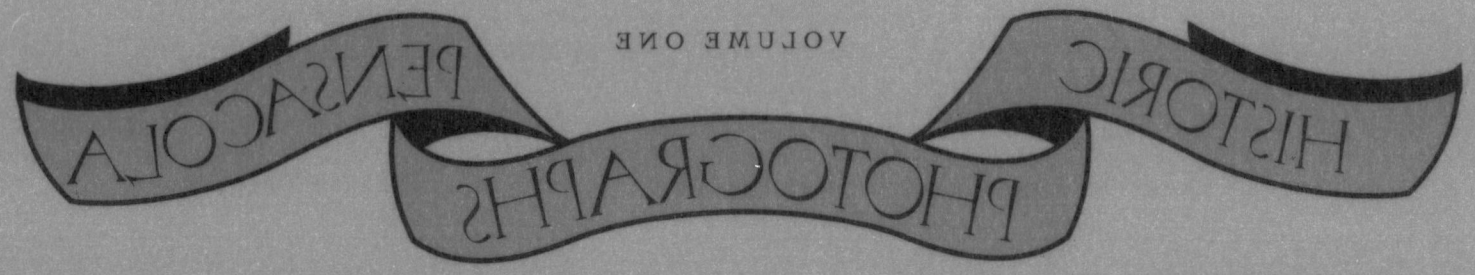

Bayshore PUBLISHING GROUP, INC.
PENSACOLA, FLORIDA

Pensacola nearing the Turn-of-the-Century. Palafox at Government Street. Circa 1894.

Published by

PENSACOLA, FLORIDA

Deborah J. Dunlap, President  Tracey L. Martin, Vice President

Post Office Box 346, Pensacola, Florida 32592-0346

1-850-434-1122

www.historicpensacola.com

© 1999 by Deborah Dunlap and Bayshore Publishing Group, Inc. Pensacola, Florida. All rights reserved.

Limited Edition First Printing 1999

Library of Congress Catalog Number: 99-068076

ISBN: 1-929727-00-3

Printed in the United States of America

Photographic selection by Deborah J. Dunlap

Digital photographic restoration and artistic design by Tracey L. Martin

Introduction by John Appleyard

Edited by Laura H. Soule

Digital film preparation by PrePress, Pensacola, Florida

VOLUME ONE

HISTORIC PHOTOGRAPHS PENSACOLA

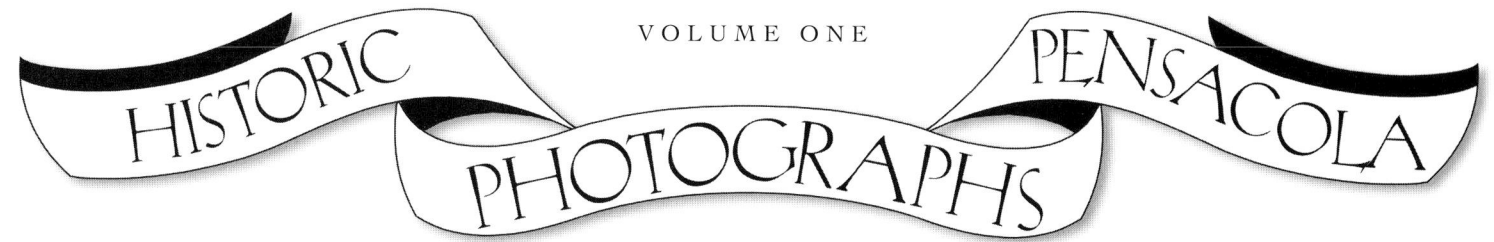

Bayshore PUBLISHING GROUP, INC.
PENSACOLA, FLORIDA

The Gulf Florida and Alabama Railroad townsite was one of many parcels of federal government land deeded to the railroad companies to encourage development. Glass negative. Circa 1910.

With love and appreciation to our families,
Ben, Devan,
Leon, Alex,
Harris and Marilyn
who believed in the ultimate success of this book
and encouraged us with their love.

The publisher gratefully acknowledges
historian John Appleyard
for his help in the preparation of this book.

Also, thanks to Laura,
Kim, Lindley, Haley
and Susie.

George W. Turton

Charles T. Cottrell and family.

The majority of photographs in this collection come from the archives of these two prominent Pensacola photographers. While we are not able to positively attribute each and every photograph to the original photographer, history tells us the late 1800 photographs were most likely taken by Mr. Turton. Mr Cottrell came to Pensacola in 1899 and lived here with his family for a half century, taking photographs of Pensacola and its people. Both photographers enjoyed national recognition and the admiration of local citizens. Their perfection of the photographic process brought serious acclaim from national judges. In a statewide photographic contest, sponsored by a national magazine, Mr. Cottrell's photograph entitled "Entrance to Pensacola Harbor" was awarded first prize in the professional division. In competition with over 3,000 prints from all over the state, Mr. Cottrell received the unanimous vote of all five judges. The photo appears on page 80 and is made from the original glass negative.

DEDICATION

In 1984, while researching her family's genealogy, Delores Pittman sought a photo of her grandfather's barber shop in downtown Milton, Florida. Her search lead her to an old concrete building on Mobile Highway in Pensacola. It was there she met aging photographer Lewis Edward Ashley.

Happy to make a sale, Mr. Ashley ushered her to a warehouse filled with cartons of century-old glass plates and fragile deteriorating plastic negatives. Mr. Ashley had purchased the personal collection of one of Pensacola's most renowned turn-of-the-century commercial photographer, Charles Cottrell and the works of late 1800's Pensacola photographer, George Turton.

On the first of what would be many visits to the Ashley Studio, Delores watched as the aging photographer made a print and then, a copy negative from one of the century-old glass negatives. He then tossed the glass into a corner, where it shattered in an unceremonious heap. Recognizing the precious historic value of what was being destroyed, Delores offered to buy the entire collection.

With Mr. Ashley's word to never break another glass negative, Delores borrowed five hundred dollars from her father for a down payment and secured a bank loan to cover the balance. For the next fifteen years, Delores lovingly preserved and restored the collection to its present glory. Working tirelessly to catalogue each negative as she produced prints, Delores plowed profits back into developing more and more of the priceless negatives.

Over the years, Delores donated copies from her collection to local historical groups and marketed prints at area art festivals. One of her greatest joys was to help people locate family photos. She would offer wisdom along with the sale. "Don't think of your purchase as just buying a photograph," she would say, "you are simply paying me to preserve your family's history."

A picture really is worth a thousand words. Thanks to this gentle, soft spoken lady, Historic Pensacola Photographs Volume One is shared with you now.

This rare glass negative shows the tunnel entrance to the Innerarity House, headquarters of the Panton-Leslie Trading Post, and St. Joseph Catholic Church in the background. Circa 1885.

CONTENTS

About the Jacket Cover:

This young couple posing at the water's edge is, most likely, the daughter and son-in-law of Turn-of-the-Century photographer, Charles T. Cottrell. Cottrell, who won national acclaim with early photographic images of Pensacola, captured the beguiling couple using a large format camera on an 8 x 10 glass negative. Circa 1913.

Photographers	6
Dedication	7
Foreward	11
Introduction	13
Logs, Lumber and Turpentine	17
Railroads	33
On The Waterfront	49
The Navy Yard	65
Downtown	81
Business Life	97
A Day In The Life	113
Forces of Nature	129
Life and Times	145

Swift Justice, Circa 1890.

FORWARD

When I purchased this collection of photographs from Delores Pittman, I had but one goal in mind — to share the stunning black and white photography with people who love the historic city I call my "adopted hometown." As I began the monumental job of choosing photos (there are over 5,000 in the collection) for this first volume, I became acutely aware of the uniqueness of having so many original glass plate negatives. As a result, it was only fitting that a book be published to tell the story of this remarkable collection.

The restoration of the glass plate negatives proved to be the most fascinating work we at Bayshore Publishing have ever done. We developed (pardon the pun) a certain reverence for the people in the photos. Enlarged on the computer screen we could look deeply into the eyes of men on the snapper smacks. We could see the determination in the eyes of the businessmen and the lumber men. We began to feel as if they were speaking directly to us from the past.

The glass negatives were not the only ones we chose for this inaugural volume. There were certain prints in the collection that begged to be included. I watched in awe as Tracey Martin enlarged a priceless 1880's George Turton photograph of a hanging. There in the photograph were two priests, most likely giving last rites to the doomed man. Standing beside them were three government officials. But most fascinating were the dozens of people lining the rooftops of the nearby buildings to watch the show.

We do not pretend to be historians, but we do love Pensacola history. The pioneer photographers of Pensacola would be pleased to know that their shutter click of a hundred years ago would capture memories that would endure into the next millennium. The memories they captured included the powerful and the private; the businessmen and the laborers; the cinch-waisted women and the washerwomen; the government buildings and the gallant military; the houses of worship and the grounds of the dead. And much, much more.

© 1999 Deborah Dunlap and Bayshore Publishing Group, Inc. Pensacola, Florida

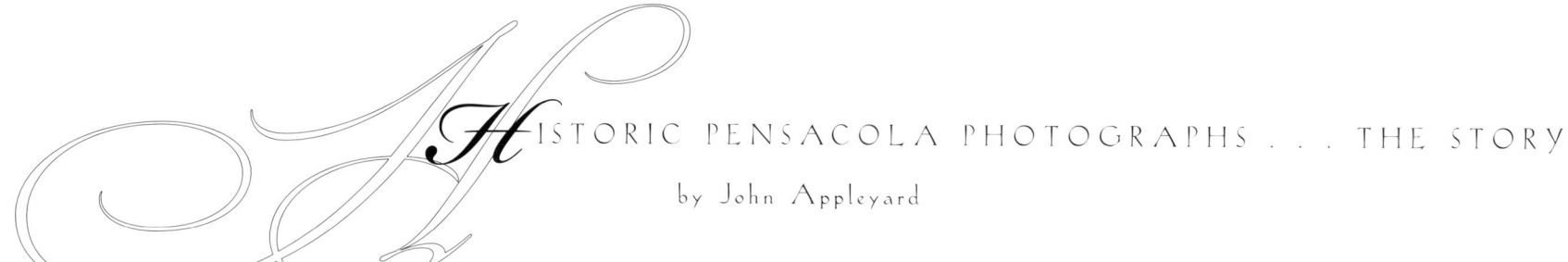

Historic Pensacola Photographs... The Story
by John Appleyard

Turning the pages of time back to 1870, and then pressing forward, Pensacola's story is unique. In fact, historians have suggested that this saga is an almost perfect microcosm of economic development experienced by chance and not through some grand plan. Because of nature's bounty, and pressing worldwide issues, what had once been a struggling seaside village was transformed into a prosperous, sophisticated community. A century ago its people reveled in their newfound wealth. Fortunately, the photographic method evolved in the years which parallel the Pensacola saga. Over time, photographers recorded and preserved many of the events, developments, activities, and even tragedies on film and glass negatives. The pages that follow illustrate a time when technical and social change figuratively exploded.

That story - in briefest form - evolved like this:

When the War Between the States ended, Pensacola's 2,000 residents slowly trickled back from their self-imposed exile. By 1870, the little city was becoming active once again, although, like most of the South, Pensacola was on its economic knees. Industries like the Navy Yard and shipping stood idle. However, over hundreds of years, nature had created a potential that had never been utilized. The region surrounding Pensacola was largely covered by yellow pine forests, most of which were untouched. This land was inexpensive, accessible, and best of all—available.

In 1870, economic conditions suddenly changed in much of Western Europe. The Industrial Revolution had begun a century ago but had developed spasmodically. Now Europe was experiencing a point where many cities required rebuilding, calling for extensive new housing for workers in the new mills and factories. The Gulf Coast area and its surrounding rich forests were the world's best available source of raw material supplies for that rebuilding. And so, the great lumbering boom began.

Within a decade, large mill companies formed throughout the area. Local docks transported timbers and finished lumber. Timbers were processed at mills on the waterfront. Hundreds of eligible workers became woodsmen. Others managed teams of oxen, operated logging railroads, or ferried rafts of logs down the Escambia River. Year after year fleets of Scandinavian sailing ships arrived in ballast and departed carrying away timbers and lumber. This traffic required longshoremen, stevedores, and other various tradesmen to service the visiting vessels and suppliers. Steadily, the Pensacola waterfront grew from a single pier to sixteen terminals. Pilots, tug boats, U.S. Customs officials, physicians, and shipping agents greeted as many as 600 vessels per year. Up and down Palafox, Baylen, Intendencia, Commendencia, and Tarragona Street, shops opened to carry on these services; places of entertainment evolved as well. By 1900, the little city by the sea had grown to a population of more than 20,000 persons.

As the new era began, the city had no railroad connection and not a single chartered bank. By the mid-1870's, those necessities took form. In 1862, retreating military forces destroyed the city's original railroad, which linked Pensacola and the Alabama border. That road reopened in 1876. The Brent and Knowles Bank opened in 1874 with other financial institutions following shortly. In 1882, the Pensacola and Atlantic Railroad, with Col. William Chipley as its director and general manager, opened to traffic to the east across the Panhandle, creating the development of that vast, but unpopulated, area. New towns arose, including Caryville, DeFuniak Springs, Holt, Bonifay, and Chipley. Agriculture flourished in the counties to the east.

With the coming of the railroad and the growth of their First National Bank, the Sullivan brothers announced they would build a new bank headquarters. It was a fine building; however, the "bank" would primarily be used as a 1,000 seat opera house. Recently created entertainment circuits operating from eastern cities now furnished talents of all kinds, and quickly a new social aura appeared: newly wealthy Pensacolians became theatergoers! Such entertainment encouraged the establishment of fine restaurants. Ladies, with money to spend but few other regular opportunities, now patronized dressmakers and newly arrived milliners, making each opera house evening gala something to behold!

By the mid-1880s, the city's original residential areas near the bay were expanding, with many successful families moving to a new district to the north. Contractors and builders such as the Turners and the Cronas designed and erected block after block of handsome homes whose features copied styles of homes in wealthy Northern centers. Fine materials came from the local lumber mills, some of which specialized in the intricate trim design making the Queen Anne house style popular. Within a decade most of the more successful families, old and new, relocated to streets near or north of Cervantes Street.

As residential neighbors relocated, commerce, churches, and centers of government followed. The churches began moving to their new locations in the mid-1870s. The first, Temple Beth-El, was completed in 1876. The Methodist Church moved to the northwest corner of Palafox and Garden in 1880, while the new Lutheran congregation built its sanctuary on Baylen at Garden Street. Likewise, St. Michael's Catholic Church and the Presbyterian Church built new facilities within the decade. St. Joseph's parish and the First Baptist Church made their movement in the 1890s, with Christ Church relocating from its 1832 site in 1903. The Norwegian Seaman's church also opened in the 1880s.

Post War Escambia County government first operated from rented stores on Government Street. To gain more permanence, property owners imposed a tax upon themselves in order to fund a fine Victorian-style courthouse and armory, which opened in 1885. The federal government built its new combined post office, customs service and courthouse at Palafox and Government streets in 1887.

Meanwhile, other economic factors were taking form. Beginning in the 1870s commercial fishing emerged as a practical industry when rail connections to the north were established; now fishermen had access to ice production and insulated rail cars. Ultimately, three companies operated fishing fleets, which plied the gulf, harvesting huge catches. Waterfront fish warehouses, icemaking plants, docks for the fleets, and railroad sidings helped to make fishing a major industry. Local firms (under such leaders as Cobb, Saunders, Warren, Welles, and Hayes) employed hundreds of men.

A growing need for naval stores arose as the fishing fleet expanded, and as more wooden sailing vessels called for lumber. Vessels required products like turpentine, pitch, gum, and rosin for caulking and sealing. The same pine trees, which provided timber, were also the source of the raw naval stores. The lumber industry expanded to employ many men for gathering rosin. Naval stores companies in Pensacola and Panama City became refiners and sales agents. In 1897, one agent alone reported exporting 40,000 barrels of turpentine and 60,000 barrels of rosin of dollar values which were huge, even for that era. All of this added to the growing waterfront community with more jobs and people.

From 1883 to 1884, three businessmen, with a city franchise, built the first phase of the much-needed streetcar system. Mule and horse-drawn cars traveled from the waterfront to the railroad depot on Wright Street. Year after year this traffic increased as routes expanded, ultimately reaching out to serve even an amusement park on the west side. In a single year more than a million passengers rode the cars.

Through the early years of its industrial boom Pensacola remained a city with few utility services. However, Pensacola became one of the first American communities with a telephone exchange, which opened in 1880. In time, as fire protection needs became increasingly obvious, city fathers borrowed funds to create a public water system, to build the first sewage collection services, and to subsidize a manufactured gas service, whose first activity was a street lighting program on downtown streets. Later, this system expanded to bring gas into homes and businesses. Near the turn of the century, new owners restructured the streetcar system, adding an electric generating plant to provide power for the cars. Privately produced electric service gradually added public services, too. By 1900, pictures of downtown streets included the tall poles that carried electric and telephone lines.

As business progressed in this largely tax-free era, many citizens transferred their earnings to savings and investments. The number and size of banks increased. The availability of capital encouraged many to invest in new business opportunities including wholesale warehousing and distribution, hotels for the visiting sales and service personnel who now came to the city, and a host of services which had not existed in 1870. Until the turn of the century, streets remained unpaved—even in 1900, only a few blocks of downtown had hard surfaces, and these with creosote blocks. Aside from the streetcars, transport was on foot, on horseback, or for the affluent, in buggies and carriages. Commercial in-town traffic primarily consisted of wagons, drays and carts. Carriage makers, horseshoers, firms to board and care for horses, harness makers, and of course shops which furnished feed for farm and domestic animals all operated downtown. By 1900, downtown had grown to include hardware stores, cigar makers, ice cream parlors, numerous drug stores, book and stationery merchants, and a variety of clothiers. By that time ready-to-wear and by-order clothing was available. Illustrating the new mechanical era, the city had a telegraph center, typewriter shops, and the popular Singer Sewing Machine headquarters.

For outdoor entertainment citizens utilized several bathhouses along the bay, on Bayou Chico, and on Lake Texar. A group of enthusiasts began a yacht club, too. Early in the new century a country club would be organized. Likewise, throughout the community, men and women enjoyed membership in such groups as Woodmen of the World, the Elks, The Moose, the Masons, the Osceola Club and a host of literary and singing societies.

A new commercial area was the heart of the growing city, bordered by Palafox, Garden, Romana, and Baylen streets. Two men jointly acquired all of this land and had in place fine office and commercial facilities. The men, attorney William Blount and banker Francis Brent, furthered the idea of expansion. Brent even had announced plans for a nine-story tower for his First national Bank. However, a great fire on October 31, 1905, destroyed much of the Blount-Brent block. The two owners promptly arranged for rebuilding, and the new seven-story Blount Building and three-story Brent Building came into being. Two years earlier Conrad Theissen had invested his savings in a five-story office building, which, at that moment, was Florida's, tallest structure.

With the completion of the Blount-Brent project downtown, Pensacola was more alive than ever. In 1908, James Muldon and his partner purchased the Methodist Church property on the corner of Garden and Palafox, razed the buildings there and erected the first phase of the Hotel San Carlos. (A second phase of the hotel would be built in 1922.) The Methodist relocated and built a fine new church on Wright Street.

Through all of these years, the largest single catalyst for growth remained the Louisville & Nashville Railroad. Its leaders, first W. D. Chipley and then, A. O. Saltmarsh, foresaw great success for the local port, far beyond lumber exports. They envisioned a canal across Nicaragua, a device which would establish Pensacola as the gateway to the Pacific and Latin America, creating markets for goods moving from Eastern and Midwestern cities. The L & N built a coal loading facility, huge double tiered warehouses, a grain elevator, and servicing rail yard near the waterfront, all of which generated employment and traffic. Furthermore, Colonel Chipley became a political figure in local and state government. All of these activities fostered additional economic optimism and growth.

And so the story continued. Along the waterfront business came and went with new ones always arriving. In 1903, the Gulf & St. Andrews Steamship Company opened and created a service employing the steamship Tarpon. This weekly operation linked Pensacola's mercantile and naval stores communities with townships to the east. In 1916, the area's first manufacturing plant opened as Newport Industries, which found ways to convert pine stumps from the cut-over forests into useful turpentine and rosin. In time, other plants located alongside Newport to utilize that firm's byproducts. By 1906, the first automobiles and trucks appeared bringing with them opportunities for expanding the city's boundaries. Ballast, which had been taken from incoming sailing ships, was used in building several square blocks of waterfront property, which later incorporated into business services. The Navy Yard, which had operated from the mid 1820's closed in 1911, to reopen three years later as the training site for naval aviation. When World War I came, that service proved a great addition to the local economy.

Through World War I and the Depression the city's economy only strengthened. New ethnic groups arrived to become part of industry and commerce. As one form of business went "out of date" another seemed to spring up in its place. Streets were paved, as were the sidewalks. Smaller marine hospitals were succeeded by the Pensacola Infirmary and St. Vincent's (owned by physicians) and then later, by the Pensacola Hospital (Sacred Heart) in 1915-16. Yellow fever was conquered, and with it Pensacola's past reputation for being unhealthy.

Happily, much of what occurred was captured on glass photographic plates and on Kodak film. Negatives and prints that survived for almost a century are now lovingly cared for by those who appreciate the city's past. This, the first volume of an anticipated series of photographic journals, includes names and dates identified to the best of current available information.

And so – welcome to the past — in North America's First Place City.

The Louisville & Nashville Union Depot at Tarragona and Wright Street. Circa 1900.

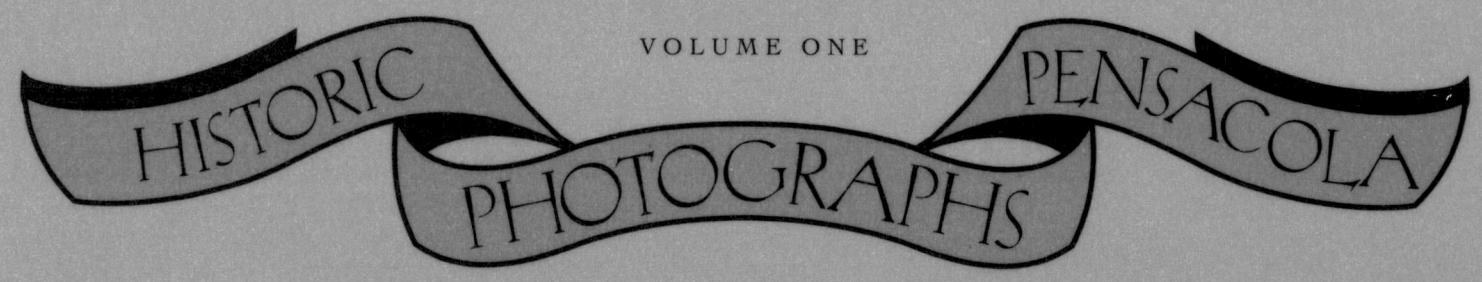

VOLUME ONE
HISTORIC PHOTOGRAPHS PENSACOLA

LOGS, LUMBER AND TURPENTINE

HISTORIC PENSACOLA PHOTOGRAPHS

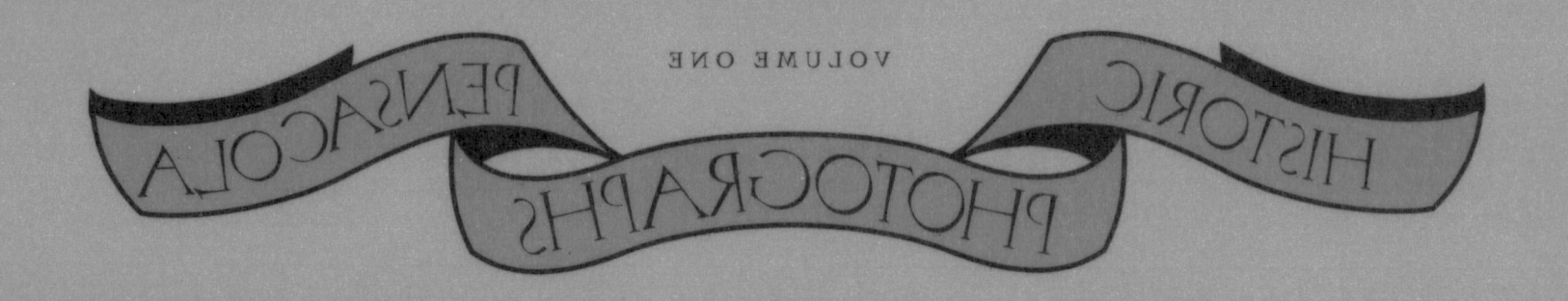

VOLUME ONE

LOGS, LUMBER AND TURPENTINE

Strong men using cross-cut saws felled thousands of acres of Northwest Florida timber. Circa 1905.

The Lindsey log wagon and a narrow guage "4 Spot" locomotive of the Skinner-McDavid Mfg. Co. Circa 1910.

McKinnons Ditch, Santa Rosa County. Logs were pulled by ox teams into manmade ditches then floated downstream to the railroad or to the river. Circa 1895.

The H.K. Porter locomotive #4 of the Muscogee Lumber Company. Circa 1895.

The W. B. Wright Company's Mill and Boom.

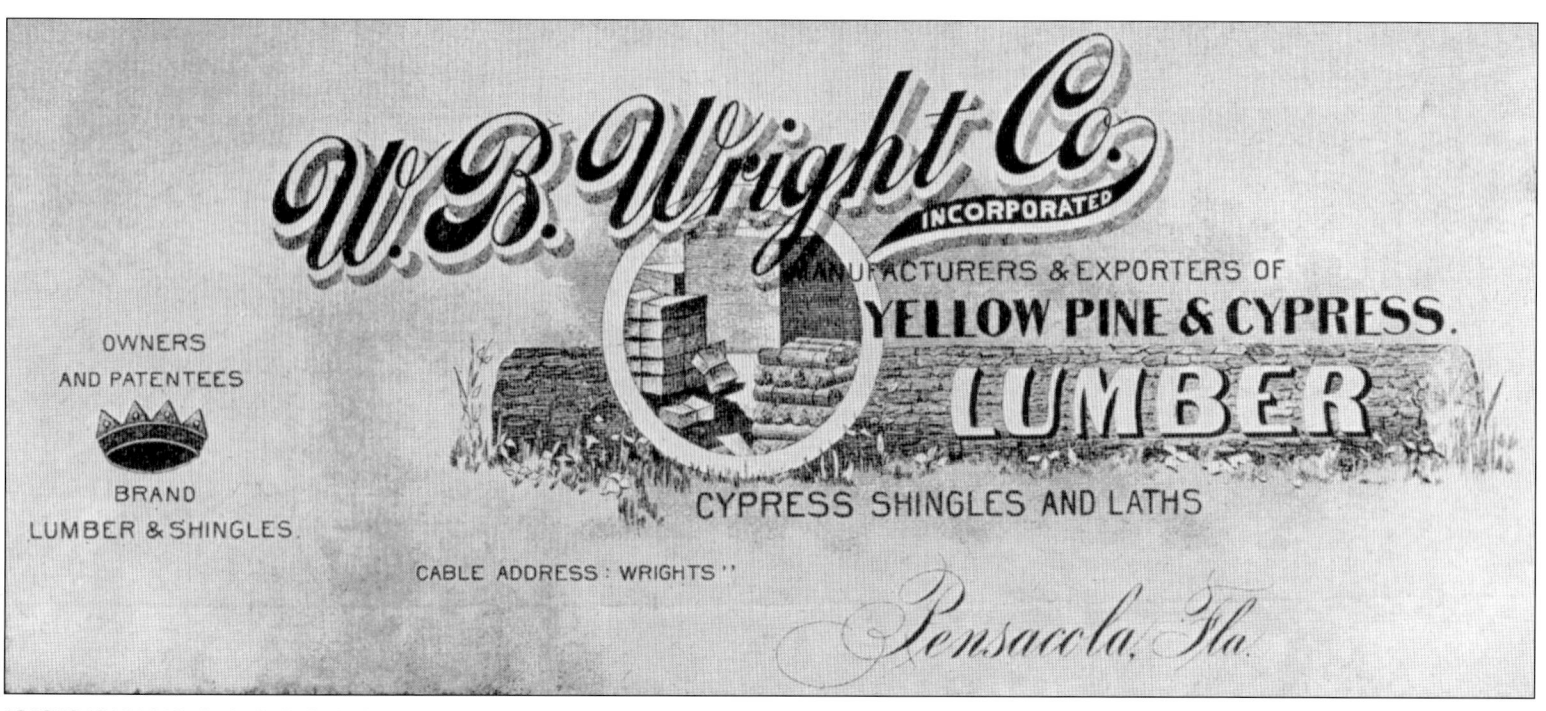

Letterhead of the W. B. Wright Co., Inc. shows the cable address, the Turn-of-the-Century equivalent to email. Circa 1900.

The Bagdad Lumber Mill was one of the largest and most profitable in Northwest Florida. Circa 1915.

The Bay Point Lumber Mill on the Garcon Peninsula. Circa 1911.

Milton waterfront businesses flourished during the lumber boom. Circa 1915.

The "Chimney" on Scenic Highway is all that remains of the Hyer-Knowles Planing Mill. Circa 1885.

A steam powered locomotive and boom move lumber on the yard of the Pensacola Creosote Company. Circa 1915.

The Pensacola Creosote Company prepared millions of board feet of cross ties to be used in building railroads. Circa 1915.

Massive timbers at the Louisville & Nashville rail yard on Tarragona Street. Circa 1925.

Bleeding the pines with a wooden ax allowed the resin to drip into buckets attached to the tree. Glass negative. Circa 1915.

The abundant Northwest Florida pine forests yeilded resin that was processed into turpentine, gum and pitch. Glass negative. Circa 1915.

Barrels of turpentine at the Consolidated Naval Stores yard. Circa 1915.

Millions of barrels of turpentine were loaded onto ships at Bagdad, Florida bound for Europe, Cuba and Latin America. Circa 1913.

HISTORIC PHOTOGRAPHS PENSACOLA

VOLUME ONE

RAILROADS

HISTORIC PENSACOLA
PHOTOGRAPHS

VOLUME ONE

RAILROADS

Railroads were a favorite subject of photographer Charles Cottrell. Glass negative. Circa 1915.

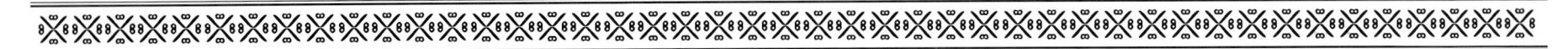

Building the Gulf Florida and Alabama Railroad. Circa 1913.

J. T. McCarthy railroad builders. Circa 1915.

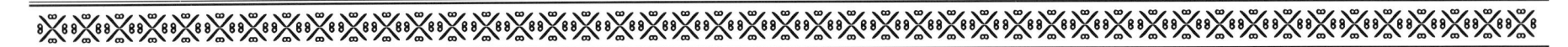

Building the bridge across the Perdido River. Glass negative. Circa 1915.

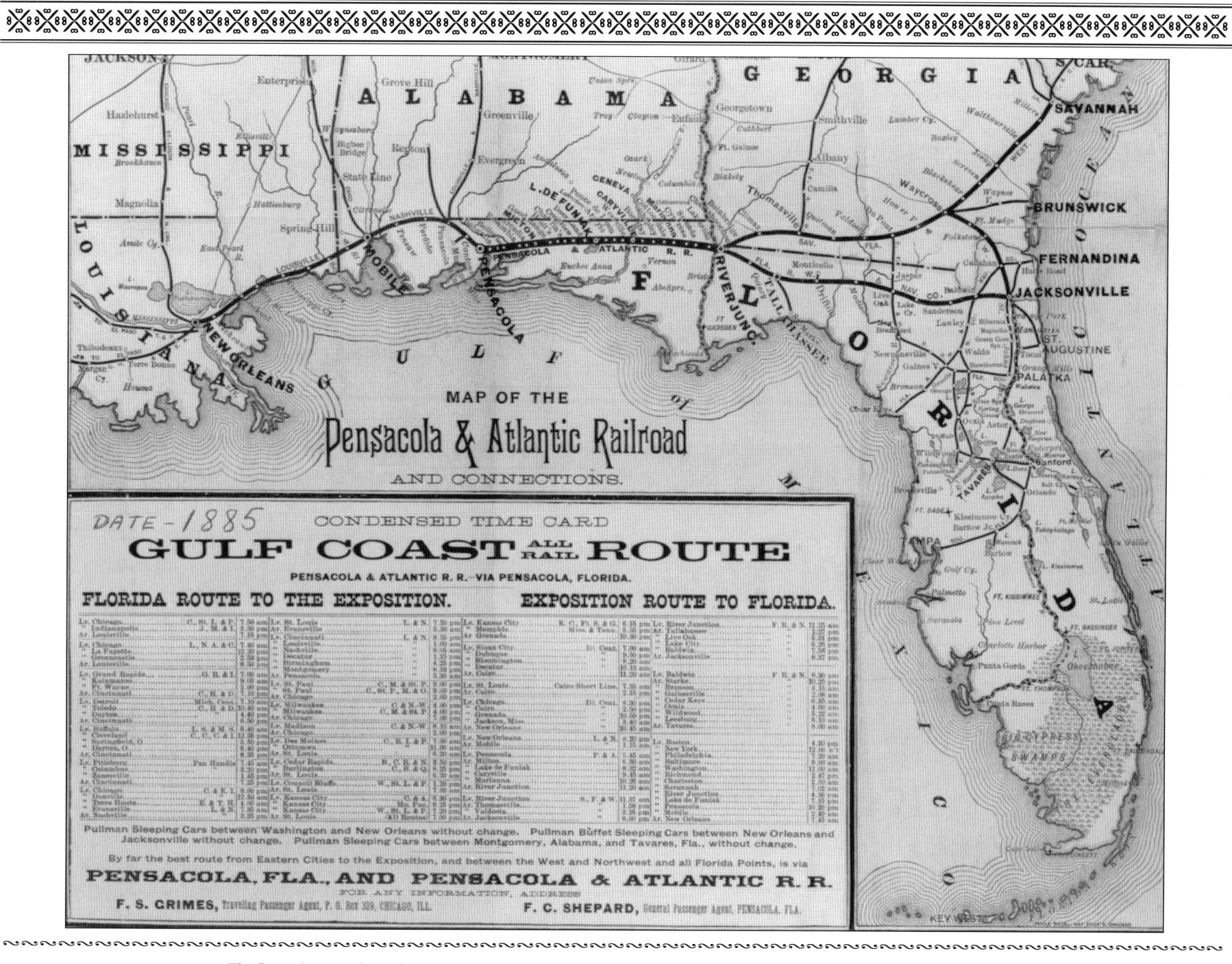

The Pensacola & Atlantic Railroad built the Victorian Union Depot in 1881. P & A was absorbed by the L & N in 1885.

The Bagdad Land and Lumber Company Railroad. Circa 1913.

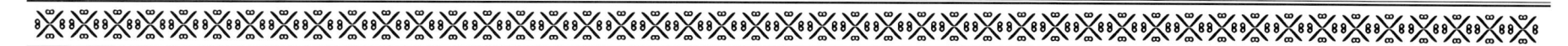

The Deep Water Route of the Gulf Florida and Alabama Railroad. Circa 1916.

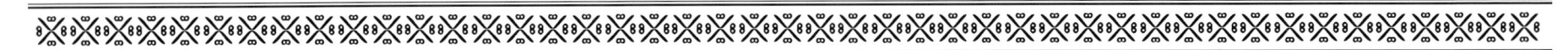

The Gulf Florida and Alabama Railroad created townsites from parcels of federal government land deeded to the railroad to encourage expansion into rural areas. Glass negative. Circa 1910.

One of the many passenger stations along the Deep Water Route. Circa 1913.

A Frisco Railroad switch engine. Circa 1915.

The Spanish mission styled Frisco passenger depot at the corner of Garden and Coyle Streets. Circa 1920.

The L & N Passenger Depot at Alcaniz and Wright Street is now the grand entrance of one of Pensacola's finest hotels. Circa 1927.

The L & N roundhouse at 10th and Wright Streets. Circa 1920.

The L & N wharf at Tarragona Street. Circa 1925.

Timber traffic at the L & N docks at Tarragona Street. Circa 1925.

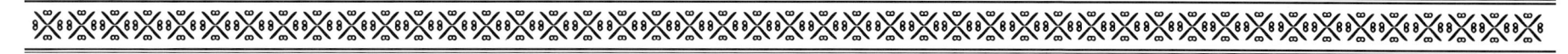

The Commendencia wharf when steam ships were beginning to replace sailing vessels. Circa 1905.

HISTORIC PHOTOGRAPHS PENSACOLA

VOLUME ONE

ON THE WATERFRONT

VOLUME ONE

HISTORIC PENSACOLA PHOTOGRAPHS

ON THE WATERFRONT

In the early part of this century Pensacola shipped fish all over the United States via refrigerated rail cars. Circa 1905.

The Warren Fish Company founded in 1880. Glass negative. Circa 1905

Catch of the day. Glass negatives. Circa 1905.

Saunders Fish and Ice Company. Circa 1910.

Captain of a Gloucester type schooner, commonly called a Snapper Smack. Glass negative. Circa 1905.

The Peerless. Glass negative. Circa 1905.

The Shamrock. Glass negative. Circa 1905.

Sternwheelers like the Choctawhatchee ferried passengers and freight. Glass negative. Circa 1905.

A calm morning. Circa 1906.

The Tarpon escaped serious damage in the 1916 hurricane (lower right photo) and was beached during the 1926 hurricane (top). She sank in a violent storm near Panama City in 1937.

A pilot boat tows a three masted schooner over the bar at Pensacola Pass. Glass negative. Circa 1900.

The long L & N wharf could handle several of the tall masted ships at one time. Circa 1903.

Unloading mahogany logs from South America at the L & N dock. Circa 1905.

Loading lumber onto ships from water pens. Glass negative. Circa 1910.

Shipping industry dry docks made necessary repairs to ships large and small. Glass negative. Circa 1915.

Imagine the sense of wonder the old fisherman felt as he watched the great flying machines over Pensacola Bay. Glass negative. Circa 1914.

HISTORIC PHOTOGRAPHS PENSACOLA

VOLUME ONE

THE NAVY YARD

VOLUME ONE

HISTORIC PENSACOLA PHOTOGRAPHS

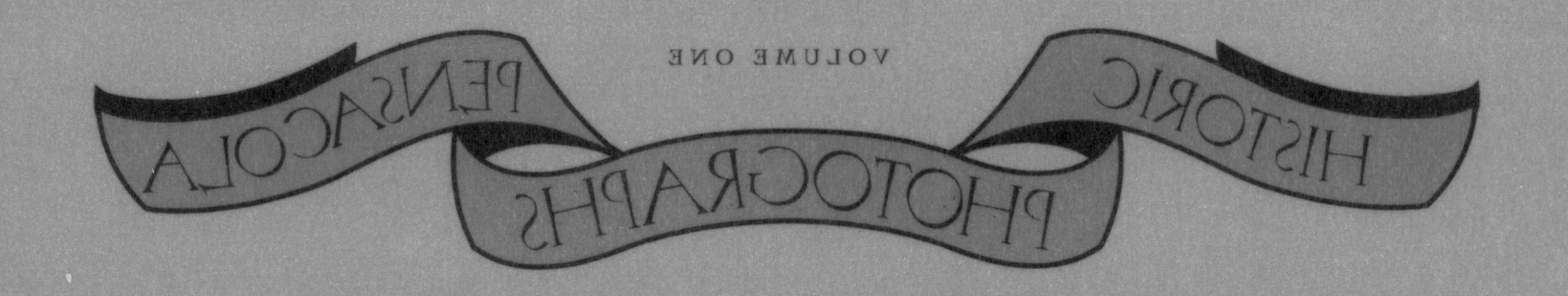

THE NAVY YARD

The Navy Lighthouse, built in 1859 is a landmark to generations of sailors. Glass negative. Circa 1920.

Armaments and anchors.

The anchor and shot park.

Navy Yard pier and lookout.

Western gate Woolsey entrance. Circa 1903.

Marine barracks.

Machine shop. Circa 1903

Black Guard unit. Circa 1903.

The birth of naval aviation. Glass negative. January 2, 1914

A Curtiss Flying Boat. Circa 1917.

The gallantry of aviators and crewmen sparked so many weddings to local debutantes that Pensacola earned the nickname "Mother-in-law of Naval Aviation." Circa 1916.

Lieutenant Richard Saufley

Lieutenant Kenneth Whiting.

Lieutenant Ellyson gives Captain Chambers a flight. Circa 1915.

Lieutenant William Corry.

Endurance tests challenged both man and machine. Glass negative. Circa 1916.

RG 72 flying boats at the Naval Aeronautic Station south shore. Circa 1916.

Women in service were volunteers and held mostly clerical jobs. Circa 1914.

U. S. Navy Aeronautics Station serviceman. Glass negative. Circa 1908.

The War Department required buildings to be camouflaged. Circa 1919.

The floating dry dock. Circa 1918

The machine shop. Circa 1918.

Machine shop crew. Circa 1918

Award winning photograph by Charles Cottrell "Entrance to Pensacola Harbor" at Pickens Point. Glass negative. Circa 1914.

VOLUME ONE

HISTORIC PHOTOGRAPHS PENSACOLA

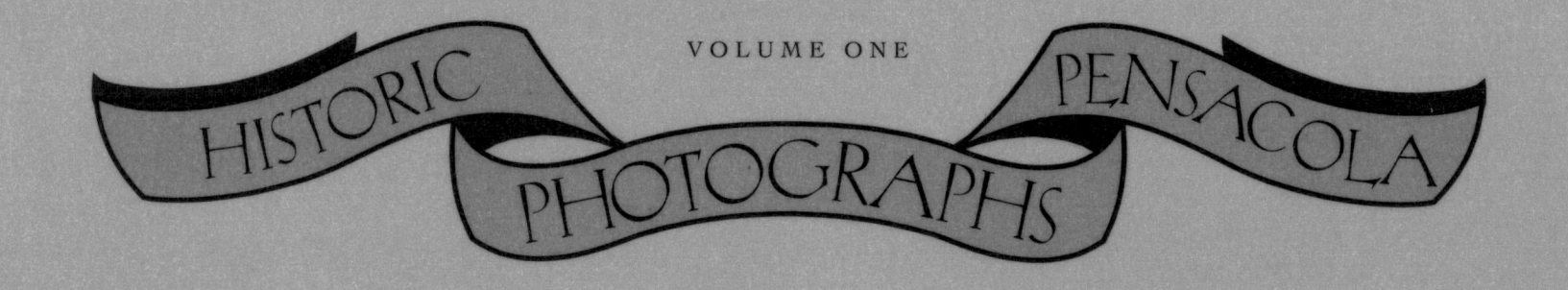

DOWNTOWN

HISTORIC PENSACOLA PHOTOGRAPHS

VOLUME ONE

DOWNTOWN

Jefferson Street, in the lower right corner, dead ends at Government Street. Circa 1929.

Garden Street between Spring and Baylen Streets. Circa 1920.

Looking east on Garden Street from the Blount building. Circa 1900.

Looking west on Government Street from the American National Bank. Circa 1913.

Looking west from the American National Bank. Circa 1913.

The U.S. Customs House and Post Office, now the Escambia County Courthouse. Circa 1900.

State militia camped on Palafox Street during the 1908 street car strike until local citizens could be deputized to preserve law and order. Glass negative.

Jefferson at Zarragoza. Circa 1913.

Plaza Ferdinand. Circa 1911.

Jackson and Devillers Street Station around 1909.

Spring Street Station around 1920.

90

A mysterious Halloween night fire in 1905 destroyed most of the south west block of Palafox at Garden.

Glass negative. Circa 1909.

Circa 1929.

Circa 1900.

The Pensacola police force posed in front of the city jail on December 12, 1909.

Belmont and Baylen Streets. Circa 1916.

Government Street at Jefferson. Circa 1925.

The Escambia County Courthouse was built in 1885 at the northeast corner of Palafox and Chase Streets at a cost of just over $44,000. Circa 1913.

People just getting off the trolley at Main Street near Palafox. Circa 1913.

VOLUME ONE

HISTORIC PHOTOGRAPHS PENSACOLA

BUSINESS LIFE

HISTORIC PENSACOLA PHOTOGRAPHS

VOLUME ONE

BUSINESS LIFE

The San Carlos Hotel was built in 1910 on the corner of Palafox and Garden. Glass negative. Circa 1920.

Elegance was the definitive word for the Hotel San Carlos. Circa 1929.

Pensacola's first radio station, WCOA broadcast from the San Carlos. Circa 1925.

Hotel guest were greeted by ornate Spanish furnishings. The grand staircase led to the elegant Hagler Ballroom. Circa 1925

The interior of the elegant First National Bank. Circa 1900.

Local businessmen were invited to inspect the new fireproof safe at the American National Bank located in the first floor of the Opera House. Circa 1903.

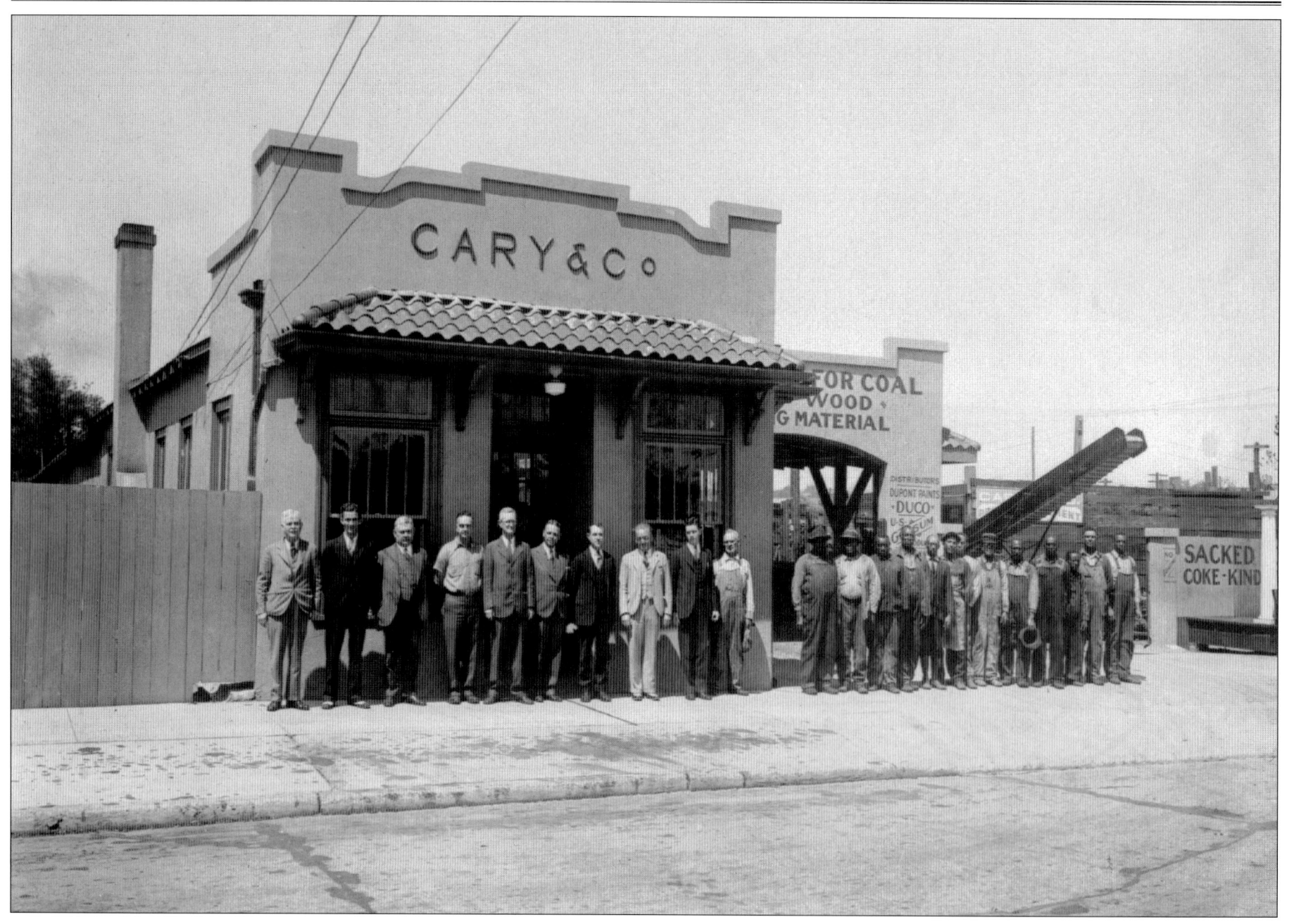

Cary & Co. was Pensacola's premier distributor of coal in the early part of the century. Circa 1929.

The Motor Inn on Gadsden and Alcaniz Streets, where area drivers enjoyed true customer service. Glass negative. Circa 1925.

Inside the B & B Restaurant on Palafox Street. Circa 1925.

T.T. Todd opened his wholesale fruit and produce company in 1919. Circa 1929.

The Coca Cola truck made frequent deliveries to neighborhood drug stores and soda fountains in the 1920's. Circa 1920 - 1929.

The Marshall Boat Works, maker of fine mahogany boats, was located on Bayou Chico. Circa 1929.

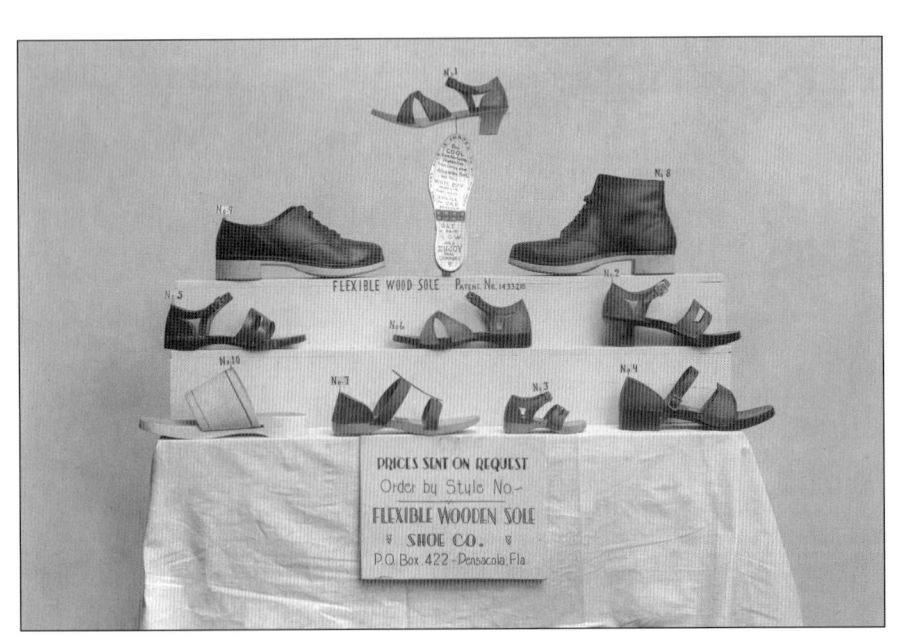

The Flexible Wooden Sole Shoe Company manufactured and sold thousands of pairs of shoes to tourists who flocked to our sandy shores. Glass negatives. Circa 1929.

Waiting for the train at the L & N Depot on Wright Street. Circa 1929.

Taking cotton to market at the L & N Freight depot. Circa 1916.

The ice plant, cold storage and offices of the Florida Power and Light company. Circa 1929.

A smooth running operation. The calendar shows February 1913. Glass negative.

The Southern Bell Telephone and Telegraph at 12 East Romana Street. Circa 1905.

The Postal-Telegraph-Cable Co. on Palafox. Circa 1916.

VOLUME ONE
HISTORIC PHOTOGRAPHS PENSACOLA

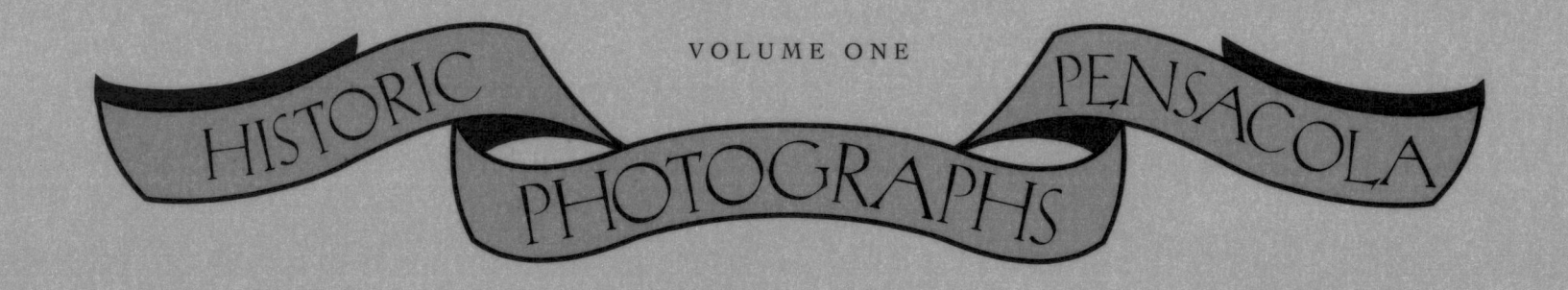

A DAY IN THE LIFE ON PALAFOX.   GLASS NEGATIVES.   CIRCA 1913

VOLUME ONE

HISTORIC PENSACOLA PHOTOGRAPHS

A DAY IN THE LIFE ON PALAFOX. GLASS NEGATIVES. CIRCA 1913

The horse and buggy was the favorite mode of transportation for the independent businessman. Palafox at Intendencia Street. Glass Negative. Circa 1913.

Life clipped along at a brisk pace. Glass negative.

But there was always time for a friendly chat. Glass negative

Business was often transacted on the sidewalk. Glass negative

The well-dressed businessman was seldom seen without a dapper hat. Glass negative.

The Pensacola economy was the talk of the state. Glass negative.

Palafox Street enjoyed a plethora of diverse storefronts. Glass negative.

Banks were strong. Spirits were high. Glass negative.

Life was good. People were happy. Glass negative.

Palafox Street was the place for shopping. Glass negative.

Well-to-do men poured fortunes into downtown buildings. Glass negative.

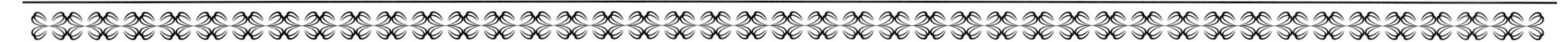

Prices were reasonable. Glass negative.

Peanuts were fresh roasted. Glass negative.

Men were good-natured. Glass negative.

Friendships were nurtured. Glass negative.

Bankers enjoyed prosperity. Glass negative.

Lawyers found plenty to do. Glass negative.

The end of a good day on Palafox Street. Glass negative. Circa 1913.

VOLUME ONE

HISTORIC PHOTOGRAPHS PENSACOLA

FORCES OF NATURE

HISTORIC PENSACOLA PHOTOGRAPHS

VOLUME ONE

FORCES OF NATURE

The foot of Barracks Street. 1906 Hurricane.

The L & N wharf. 1906 Hurricane.

Barcelona Street. 1906 Hurricane.

Main Street at Jefferson. 1906 Hurricane.

Baylen Slip. 1906 Hurricane. Glass negative.

Barracks Street. 1906 Hurricane.

Looking north on Palafox from Romana Street. 1906 Hurricane.

The Pensacola Boat Club on Bayou Chico. 1906 Hurricane.

The Runyan home on Bayou Chico. 1906 Hurricane.

The sternwheeler "Eugene" at the Baylen Street wharf. 1906 Hurricane.

Muscogee wharf. 1916 Hurricane.

Generations of Pensacolians paid the high price of living in paradise. 1916 Hurricane.

The Palafox pier awash in a sea of timber. 1916 Hurricane.

The L & N wharf. 1926 Hurricane.

The Pensacola Yacht Club boat at the Bayou Chico Bridge. 1926 Hurricane.

In the distance is Old Christ Church, a solid reminder that God is with us. 1926 Hurricane.

VOLUME ONE

HISTORIC PHOTOGRAPHS PENSACOLA

LIFE AND TIMES

VOLUME ONE

HISTORIC PENSACOLA PHOTOGRAPHS

LIFE AND TIMES

Old Christ Church on Adams Street. Circa 1900.

Immanuel Lutheran Church on the northeast corner of Garden and Baylen. Circa 1885.

St. Michaels Catholic Church on Palafox. Circa 1887.

Presbyterian Church. Glass negative. Circa 1905.

Methodist Church on Palafox and Garden. Circa 1890.

Christ Episcopal Church on Wright Street. Circa 1917.

Presbyterian Church on Chase Street. Circa 1905.

Norwegian Seaman's Church on South Palafox. Circa 1905.

First Methodist Church on Wright Street. Circa 1925.

St. Katherine Episcopal Church on Cervantes near 6th Street. Circa 1905.

First Baptist Church on Palafox at Jackson Street. Circa 1905.

Temple Bethel on Chase Street. Circa 1890.

Public School No. 1 on Wright Street. Circa 1890.

Olive School. Circa 1890.

Industrial Normal Institute. Glass negative. Circa 1910.

A. V. Clubbs School. Circa 1920.

Principal Ali Yniestra with teachers at Hallmark School. Circa 1910.

Hallmark School on South E Street. Circa 1925.

Pensacola High School. Circa 1910.

Pensacola High School at Lee Square. Glass negative. Circa 1922.

Pensacola Athletic Club at Baylen and Belmont. Circa 1880.

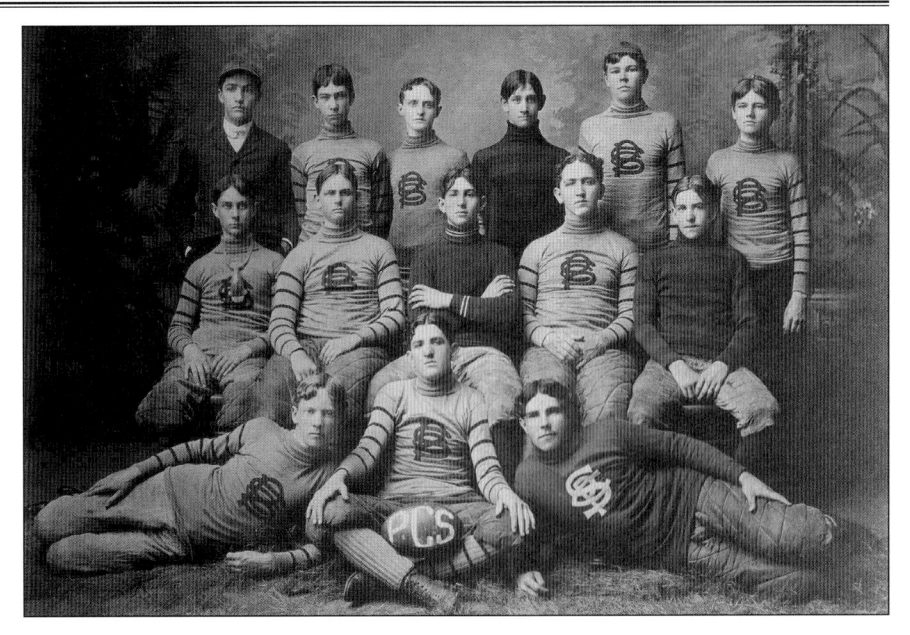

Pensacola Classical School. Circa 1890.

Bankers Basketball team. Circa 1927

Pensacola Flyers baseball team. Circa 1909.

Pensacolians enjoyed dramatic stage productions at the Opera House. Circa 1913.

The latest in tools and machinery at the Pensacola Fair. Circa 1909.

July 4th parade in downtown Milton. Circa 1916.

An upper class home in North Hill. Circa 1910.

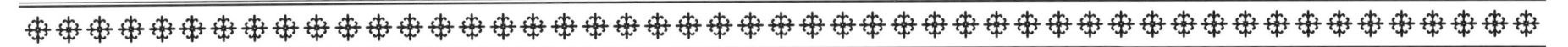

Hunters show off their catch in front of City Hall. Glass Negative. Circa 1913.

Some prey proved more elusive than others. Glass negative. Circa 1913.

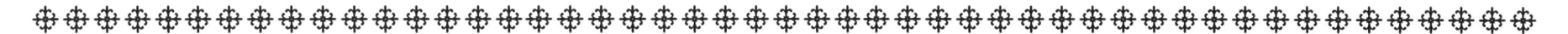

Beach swings on Gulf Breeze peninsula. Glass negative. Circa 1913.

A day at the beach. Circa 1900.

Taking Father to the beach. Glass negative. Circa 1900.

Gulf Breeze outing. Glass negative. Circa 1900.

A basket for shade. Glass negative. Circa 1900.

Another day in Paradise. Glass negative. Circa 1900.

Camp Jouart, Gulf Breeze peninsula. Glass negative. Circa 1900.

Gone fishing. Glass negative. Circa 1913.

Island home at Bayou Texar entrance. Glass negative. Circa 1913.

Crabbing near the shore. Glass negative. Circa 1913.

An interesting catch. Glass negative. Circa 1913.

Bayview Park. Glass negative. Circa 1913.

Boat races at Bayview Park. Circa 1927.

Saccaro Bath House. Glass Negatives. Circa 1913.

The Pensacola Yacht Club on Palafox Street. Circa 1913.

Fish Class boats in a GYA regatta on Pensacola Bay. Glass negative. Circa 1920.

The W. S. Keyser home became the Pensacola Country Club. Glass negative. Circa 1923.

Golfing in Pensacola in the early part of the century. Circa 1906.

A. C. Blount II as King Priscus of Mardi Gras. Circa 1900.

The first Mardi Gras parade of the 20th Century on Palafox Street. Circa 1900.

Prominent families participated in the festive parades. Glass negative. Circa 1917.

And the beat goes on. Palafox between Intendencia and Romana Streets. Circa 1916.